A souvenir guide

Overbeck's
Devon

G000117194

National Trust

A Home with a View

Perched on a shelf high above the Salcombe Estuary, Overbeck's looks down across the coastline. Originally known as Sharpitor after a craggy outcrop of rock nearby known as Sharp Tor, it was one of the first houses to be erected in the area by a local builder, Mr Albert Stumbles, in the late 19th century.

In 1901 Edric Hopkins bought Sharpitor along with two further acres of land, and was responsible for laying out much of the garden in its present form and cultivating tender plants. He lived there until 1913 when the property was sold to Captain George Medlicott Vereker who had a great love of gardening. Because the Verekers felt the existing house was too small, they rebuilt the present house on the same site, facing the sea.

The building of the house was completed just before the outbreak of the First World War when it became a Red Cross convalescent home for soldiers. One of the builders of the house, Gunner Servington Hodder, later became a patient there.

Bequeathed to the National Trust

Otto Overbeck bought the house for his retirement in 1928 and lived there until his death in 1937, when he left the house and garden to the National Trust, stipulating that it should be renamed Overbeck's in his memory. Part of the house is now a museum which is as full of the unexpected as Overbeck himself. The house is also partly used by the Youth Hostels Association.

Above The house today

Left Overbeck's formerly known as Sharpitor, 1912

A cosmopolitan collector

Although he was born in England, Otto Christoph Joseph Gerhardt Ludwig Overbeck was descended from a distinguished Dutch family. His parents were of mixed nationality: his father, Joseph, was Dutch and Italian, his mother Prussian and French. Perhaps this cosmopolitan background accounted for his varied interests.

A man of many talents

A research chemist by profession, he was also an accomplished linguist, artist and inventor, and, as you will see, an avid collector. He was also an accomplished fisherman and had a record for catching a 17lb carp from Croxby Pond in Lincolnshire in 1902, the largest ever recorded at that date.

Take a look at the display of Otto Overbeck's inventions. Whilst working as a research chemist he was employed at a Grimsby brewery where he developed a non-alcoholic beer, but it was never commercially produced because the government insisted on levying a tax on it.

Above Otto Overbeck demonstrating his electrical rejuvenator on himself, by Leonard Rosoman, 1990 (National Trust Foundation for Art)

Left Self-portrait of Otto Overbeck, 1902

Stay young and beautiful

Otto Overbeck's most successful invention was the 'electrical rejuvenator' that he patented in the 1920s, and which he claimed could defy the ageing process if users applied the electrodes from his device to their skin. He produced various pamphlets and books on his 'electrical theory of life', and successfully marketed the rejuvenator worldwide. Otto Overbeck once said, 'My age is 64 years but I feel more like a man of 30'.

You can judge for yourself Otto Overbeck's youthful looks by his self-portrait on the wall.

'Since completing my apparatus and using it on myself, I have practically renewed my youth.'

Otto Overbeck on his electrical rejuvenator, 1925

Mr Otto C. J. G. L. Overbeck

On the last day of May there passed away one who, if he could not be considered a great gardener, was at least deeply interested in the craft. Readers of 'Gardening Illustrated' will, I know, grieve to hear the death of Mr Overbeck, with whose name they will be familiar from the frequent notes in these pages of the rare and tender plants which it has been my privilege to collect from his gardens at Sharpitor, near Salcombe. He did much to improve them and to add to their extent.

By profession an analytical chemist, he was known to a far wider public by advertisements in the daily press of the rejuvenating machine he had invented. He was keenly interested in all branches of natural history, and a great collector. Indeed, to his passion for collecting we owe so much of the interest in the gardens at Sharpitor. Here may be seen many species of Acacia and Eucalyptus and all sorts of Fuchsias, all growing and perfectly happy in the open air. He was also interested in Succulents, and took a pride in showing to visitors the huge plants of Cactus growing in the garden.

Mr Overbeck died of a painful illness, which luckily was not of a very long duration. Though he used to say that by means of his rejuvenation machine he intended to live till he was 126, he passed away when he was only 77.

Extract from Otto Overbeck's obituary (May 1937)

Tour of the House

Marvel at the fascinating and diverse range of exhibits, with rooms devoted to natural history, local maritime history, children's toys and Otto Overbeck's own family heirlooms.

The Staircase Hall and Landing

As you enter the museum, you will see that the handsome mahogany staircase is the central focus to the hall.

Mechanical melodies

This extraordinary music box (dating from the 1890s) is now one of our most popular exhibits. Otto Overbeck was in the local Malborough pub, saw it playing, and was so fascinated that he made a deal with the landlord to swap it for a modern gramophone and a £5 note.

Polyphons were built in Leipzig, Germany, but because of heavy import duty, the Manchester firm of Gouldman bought only the mechanical parts, which were then fitted into English-made cabinets. Rotating metal discs with projecting pins strike a star-wheel which plucks two metal combs, the teeth of which are tuned to a different note – you may be surprised how clear the tunes sound.

We play the polyphon at regular intervals throughout the day. As we are unable to use the older discs because of their poor condition, we are replacing them with new ones. When you hear the music, perhaps you would like to make a donation towards one of these. A CD of the tunes played on the polyphon is available in the shop.

Left The Staircase Hall

Opposite The polyphon

Among the pictures hanging in this room is a later version of a portrait dated 1560 of Cosimo de' Medici, the first Grand Duke of Tuscany (1519–74). Overbeck's father, Joseph, may have acquired it while working at the Vatican in Rome.

A room within a room

Within this room is a reconstructed cottage parlour dating to the late 19th century. The range was manufactured by Lidstone's, a Kingsbridge foundry. The two Windsor chairs were also made in the West Country, but the late 19th-century clock is from America. Standing on the carved elm chest is a harvest barrel used to carry beer or cider into the fields.

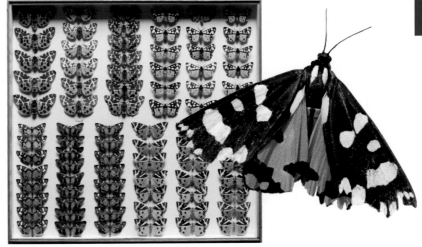

Life through a lens

The photographs on the walls and in the albums on the centre table are the work of local photographer Edward Chapman (1850–1939), taken around 1900. You can see a collection of photographic equipment, including the Thornton Pickard camera used by Chapman, in the Overbeck's Room.

All creatures great and small

On the landing you will see examples of Otto Overbeck's natural history collection, which includes stuffed animals and birds, birds' eggs, fish, fossils, shells and insects. Assembled in the late 19th century, it represents a typical Victorian collection.

Today we still 'collect' wildlife but in a different way to that of the Victorians. We encourage wildlife into our gardens and enjoy preserving it in photographs and films.

Have a look at our 'Gateway to the Countryside' display for information about local wildlife walks, and please use our microscopes to take a closer look at bugs and plants.

Above left Joseph Overbeck, Otto's father

Above Collection of pinned-out scarlet tiger moths (*Callimorpha dominula*)

Above right A live scarlet tiger moth (*Callimorpha dominula*)

The Maritime Room

The Maritime Room celebrates Salcombe's past as a prosperous port. The scale models, paintings and photographs record ships that were built, sailed and lost in these waters.

A dangerous trade

The port of Salcombe was at its peak during the 1870s, when as many as 95 ocean-going vessels were using the haven. These ships plied a particularly arduous trade, leaving Salcombe for Cadiz, where they took on salt destined for Newfoundland. This cargo would then be exchanged for salt cod and shipped on to the Mediterranean where it would be exchanged again for fruit before returning home. Many of these schooners were built in Salcombe, and you can see examples of the tools used in the shipbuilding trade around the room.

Above The ship's wheel from the *Herzogin Cecilie* (now on display at NT Bradley Manor)

Left The *Herzogin Cecilie*

Below Model ships and nautically themed paintings in the Maritime Room

For those in peril

The best-known wreck along this coastline is the *Herzogin Cecilie*, a Finnish tall four-masted barque which regularly took part in the Grain Races prior to the Second World War. In 1936, she won the race and then moored at Falmouth. Continuing the voyage, she hit the Ham Stone near Soar Mill Cove in fog, and sank. The story of the *Herzogin Cecilie* is told in the album on the counting house desk. Only a model of her tensioning shackle and chain link is on display due to the original becoming very delicate.

Hanging on the wall is a picture of the *Restless*, a Salcombe trading vessel which was painted by one of the most prolific of British ship portraitists, Reuben Chappell (1870–1940). In 1814 the *Restless* was in a collision with another ship in the River Thames, and she sank with the sad loss of three of her crew.

One of the first schooners built in Salcombe was the *Phoenix*, a painting of which hangs in this room along with two portraits of her master, William Port. Built in 1836, the *Phoenix* led an active trading life until 1842, when she set sail from Cardiff bound for Barcelona; neither ship nor crew were heard of again.

HMS *Captain* was an early example of a turret warship, powered by both sail and steam. Her design was the brainchild of naval officer Captain Cowper Coles. However, while still on its trials in April 1870, the ship capsized with the tragic loss of almost all the 500 crew.

A family affair

The large oak desk in the centre of the room came from the counting house of Shipping Agents G.C. Fox of Falmouth, where hand-written ledgers would record ship movements. The company originated in 1762 and closed down in 2003.

Honesty pays

On top of the desk are two brass tobacco machines patented by Rich of Bridgwater in the early 19th century. A coin would release the button to open the lid for the smoker to remove a plug of tobacco. The boxes were also known as honesty boxes, because it was possible to take more than your share from the machine.

Did you know?
At low tides the *Herzogin Cecilie's* deck and mizzenmast can still be seen in Starehole Bay. In the display case is a fragment of the first telegraph cable laid between England and France. It came ashore at Starehole Bay, where foundations of the old engine cottage can still be seen.

The Overbeck's Room

This room originally housed a library. Today it is still home to the three magnificent leather-bound volumes on Roman antiquities. These were written and illustrated by Otto Overbeck's ancestor, Dutch painter Bonaventura van Overbeke, in the late 17th century. The volumes were published in 1708 by Michael van Overbeke under the patronage of Queen Anne, whose insignia adorn the covers, when Michael was the Dutch Ambassador to England.

Dolls

In another cabinet you will find a collection of 19th-century dolls. Notice how dolls from this period often resembled adults rather than children; baby dolls did not become popular until the 1880s. Novelty dolls were also made, like the German example, with a revolving head to show one face sleeping, one crying and the last smiling.

The collection of dolls in national dress was made by Miss Irene Ellis and includes a pair of dolls resembling an elderly Chinese couple. Such dolls would probably have been given to children attending a missionary school.

Right A 19th-century French doll

Shells and scrimshaw

Shell collecting was popular during the 18th and 19th centuries. Shells on display in the cabinet come mainly from the Americas and Australia. They would have been brought back by sailors who would also have painted the ostrich eggs and decorated the sperm-whale teeth, a folk art of fashioning objects from or engraving pictures on bone or ivory known as scrimshaw.

Many of the other curios were collected by Otto Overbeck, including the armadillo handbag.

The Secret Room

Hidden under the stairs, the Secret Room has been specially created by the National Trust for children and is full of toys. There are room settings from dolls' houses which belonged to the Overbeck family. Fred the ghost can often be found hiding in the Secret Room, where he loves to play among the toys.

Did you know?
The rocking horse was given to Salcombe School in 1890. The best pupil of the week was allowed to ride the horse for fifteen minutes.

Above right Engraved sperm whale teeth featuring images of a sailor and his sweetheart

Below right An ostrich egg painted with a tropical theme

From a Home to a Hospital (1915–1919)

In memory of their second son, Second Lieutenant Robert Vereker, 2nd Battalion Grenadier Guards, who was killed in the retreat from Mons, Belgium on 25 August, just 22 days into the war, at the age of 21, Captain and Mrs Vereker offered their new home to the Red Cross Society. It was to be used rent free as a Voluntary Aid Hospital for the treatment of convalescent British and allied troops.

Below Soldiers and nurses outside Sharpitor VA Hospital

Volunteer for victory

Sharpitor VA Hospital formally opened on 21 May 1915, and was run entirely by volunteers, including the Verekers. It was supported by a constant flow of gifts, both financial and in kind, from the local community. Bed numbers were increased in 1915 from 24 to 40. Voluntary Aid Detachments were created to provide additional aid to the Territorial Forces Medical Service and volunteers known as VADs performed nursing and first-aid duties. VADs were often middle-class women eager to 'do their bit'. They undertook a short course for which a certificate was awarded.

The 'soldier's smoke'

The spirits of the soldiers were kept high with home-produced entertainment including concerts, plays, boat trips, picnics, whist drives and billiard matches. The *Kingsbridge Gazette* reported in 1915 that special thanks were due for the magnificent gift of 10,000 cigarettes from the Agent General for Victoria and his daughter, Miss Cath McBride.

Fifteen brides for fifteen soldiers

By the time of its closure on 29 January, 1919, 1,020 convalescents had passed through 'The Old Home' as it was affectionately known, and thanks to all the skill and untiring dedication of the staff not a single death was recorded. However, fifteen men departed with the addition of a bride from the neighbourhood!

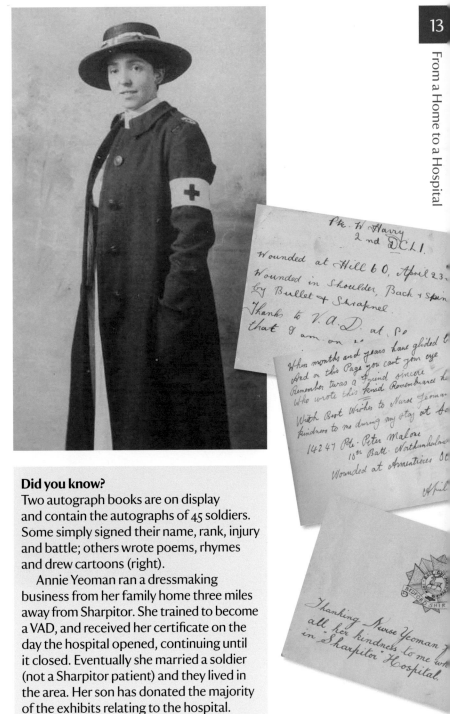

Did you know?
Two autograph books are on display and contain the autographs of 45 soldiers. Some simply signed their name, rank, injury and battle; others wrote poems, rhymes and drew cartoons (right).

Annie Yeoman ran a dressmaking business from her family home three miles away from Sharpitor. She trained to become a VAD, and received her certificate on the day the hospital opened, continuing until it closed. Eventually she married a soldier (not a Sharpitor patient) and they lived in the area. Her son has donated the majority of the exhibits relating to the hospital.

Above **Nurse Annie Yeoman**

Hidden history

For Better or Worse

Love was in the air when Salcombe sisters Dorothy and Gladys Rundle met two Canadian servicemen who were convalescing at Sharpitor House during the First World War. The hospital opened in August 1915 and was run by volunteers, supported by gifts from the local community.

Dorothy married Bill De'Roit and Gladys became Mrs Jack Anderson, and both couples settled in Canada, where they each had a son and a daughter.

Tragedy struck in the Second World War when Gladys and Jack's son Bill, a 21-year-old flying officer in the Royal Canadian Air Force, was killed when his Halifax bomber came down in this country in November 1944.

Extract from *The Kingsbridge Gazette*, 2009

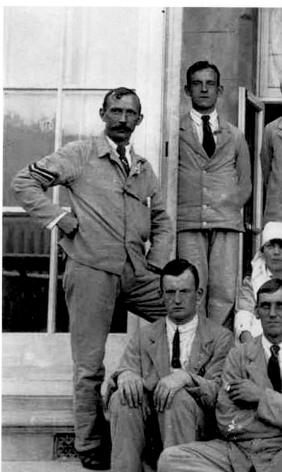

Top Bill and
Dorothy De'Roit

Above Jack and
Gladys Anderson

Shop and Tea-room

When the house was used as a hospital, the present tea-room was originally the soldiers' billiard room. The shop was Otto's studio where he carried out most of his work. The room retains many of its original features including the wooden panelling and decoration on the walls. Above the fireplace is a painting of Otto in his garden which was painted by Leonard Rosoman.

We still enjoy a warm fire in the colder months, so kick off those boots and warm your toes!

Above Soldiers playing billiards whilst convalescing at Sharpitor during the First World War

Left Group of soldiers outside Sharpitor Hospital

Wildlife spotter

Slow worm
(*Anguis fragilis*)

Convolvulus hawkmoth
(*Agrius convolvuli*)

Adder (male)
(*Vipera berus*)

Peregrine falcon
(*Falco peregrinus*)

Smooth newt
(*Triturus vulgaris*)

Firecrest
(*Regulus ignicapillus*)

Speckled wood butterfly
(*Pararge aegeria*)

Great spotted woodpecker
(*Dendrocopos major*)

Nuthatch
(*Sitta europaea*)

Emperor dragonfly
(*Anax imperator*)

Greater horseshoe bat
(*Rhinolophus ferrumequinum*)

Humming bird hawkmoth
(*Macroglossum stellatarum*)

Grey wagtail
(*Motacilla cinerea*)

Elephant hawkmoth
(*Dielephila elpenor*)

Poplar hawkmoth caterpillar
(*Laothoe populi*)

Grass snake
(*Natrix natrix*)

Wildlife on our doorstep

How we encourage different species into our gardens

We recycle clippings and other green waste in the compost area which is then returned to the soil as mulch and fertilizer – enjoy a demonstration about how we do this.

We collect rain water from the roofs and use it to irrigate the garden and the greenhouse.

Because we rely upon the weather to provide all our water for the garden we will not use tap water for watering. This is extremely worthwhile although it can sometimes leave us a little vulnerable in times of drought.

To ensure there is habitat for wildlife we place small piles of old logs in out-of-the-way corners of the garden that make good homes for hedgehogs and beetles. By leaving grass longer in some areas we also attract invertebrates (animals without backbones e.g. worms, snails and insects).

Look up and you may see one of a number of bird houses, bee homes and bat boxes that we have placed in the garden. Our bee house encourages native species which usually live a solitary life (unless in the mating season) and live in small crevasses in the walls or in old timber, represented in the picture. One species attracted to our garden is the red mason bee (*Osmia rufa*).

Many different types of flowering plants are grown at Overbeck's providing valuable food for birds and insects throughout most of the year.

Above **Hedgehog**
Below left **Bee home**

Attracting wildlife

Peacock butterfly (*Inachis io*) on buddleia (*Buddleja davidii*)

Fleabane (*Inula magnifica*)

Early bumble bee (*Bombus pratorum*)

Painted lady (*Cynthia cardui*) on red valerian (*Centranthus rubber*)

Grape hyacinth (*Muscari latifolium*)

Tortoishell butterfly (*Aglaisurticae*) on ice plant (*Sedum spectabile*)

Toothpick weed (*Ammi visnaga*)

Opium poppy (*Papaver 'Lauren's Grape'*)

Large white butterfly (*Pieris brassicae*) on dahlia

Brazilian verbena (*Verbena bonariensis*)

Hoverfly (*Criorhina berberina*)

Comma butterfly (*Polygonia c-album*) on knautia

Holly blue butterfly (*Celastrina argiolus*)

Silver-washed fritillary butterfly (*Argynnis paphia*)

Garden speedwell (*Veronica longifolia*)

Gentian sage (*Salvia patens 'Cambridge blue'*)

Exotic plant spotter

Ginger lily *(Hedychium densiflorum 'Assam Orange')*

Crimson bottlebrush *(Callistemon citrinus)*

Poor man's umbrella *(Gunnera manicata)*

Earring flower *(Fuchsia boliviana)*

Parrot lily *(Alstroemeria psittacina)*

Amicia *(Amicia zygomeris)*

Flowering maple *(Abutilon x hybridum)*

Lantern tree *(Crinodendron hookeranum)*

African blue lily *(Agapanthus 'Headbourne' hybrid)*

Sun bromeliad *(Fascicularia bicolor)*

Chinese dogwood *(Cornus kousa)*

Tower of jewels *(Echium pininana)*

Tree fern *(Dicksonia antarctica)*

Angel's trumpet *(Brugmansia sanguine)*

Tulip tree *(Liriodendron tulipifera)*

Red hot poker *(Kniphofia 'Victoria')*

A Piece of the Mediterranean

Located just above the Salcombe Estuary, the favourable climate, with its mild winters enjoyed on this southerly stretch of the coast, has allowed an extraordinary garden with a strong Mediterranean influence to develop.

The warm microclimate encourages rare and tender plants to flourish and it looks further afield for inspiration not only from the Mediterranean but also from Africa, to the Far East, to South America and New Zealand. This is in keeping with the long tradition of growing an extending range of unusual and exotic plants here, which are not often found living outdoors in England.

Edric Hopkins, the first owner, laid out much of the garden structure, creating a series of small enclosures and broad terraces, building the walls and castellations from the grey rock which was excavated and recovered from the cliff side. The Verekers continued to diversify the plantings, and were followed by Otto Overbeck in 1928, who believed he had found the perfect place to give free reign to his fascination with the exotic and sub-tropical.

What is a microclimate?
A microclimate is the distinctive climate of a small-scale area, such as a garden, park, valley or part of a city. The weather in a microclimate may change suddenly or unpredictably, such as temperature, rainfall, wind or humidity, and may be slightly different to the conditions prevailing over the area as a whole.

Opposite Ellis Manley, Head Gardener 1961

Below Otto Overbeck in his garden; painted by Leonard Rosoman (National Trust Foundation for Art)

'It is so warm and beautiful here. I grow Bananas, Oranges and Pomegranates in the open garden, and have 3,000 palm trees, planted out in my woods and garden.'

Otto Overbeck's letter to a friend, 1933

A man for all seasons

With all good gardens there is usually a dedicated team, and when Otto Overbeck owned the property Ellis Manley was his gardener. He would have the same tasks and difficulties when gardening such a unique garden as our garden team today, however we do have access to a larger range of information and expertise than perhaps existed in those days. Imagine finding out how to grow these new and wonderful species, when for many they had never seen such plants. We are lucky enough to have some of the books about plants and gardening that Ellis Manley used and some that were presented to him by Otto Overbeck, which can be seen in the museum. Our garden team is as dedicated today as it was in Otto Overbeck's time to ensure it is kept for future generations to appreciate.

Love me tender, love me true

Rare and tender plants were favoured from the beginning, and more than 100 years later some of these are still flourishing.

It is an informal garden, with adventurous planting throughout. There are bold foliage contrasts, with luxuriant leaves set against the spikes of yuccas and agaves, complemented by rich swathes of hot colours in the long summer months. Wandering around the garden, it soon becomes clear that there are surprises around most corners.

From the flagpole in front of the house, where Otto Overbeck's flag with the coat of arms is usually flying, there is a wonderful view looking down the estuary towards Salcombe, one of the many maritime vistas that the garden offers. Turning to your right, take the rising path leading away from the house. Follow this path until you come to a garden on a level, with four large flower beds.

The Statue Garden

Once the site of a tennis court, this area is now dominated by lush plantings of tender perennials, including a good range of salvias, agapanthus and cannas, as well as kniphofias, inulas and heleniums. These are complemented by unusual annuals, wherever space allows. The Statue Garden is filled with colour and fragrance from early June through to the end of the autumn, and is a rich source of food for the many bees and butterflies that frequent it.

Trees are the best antiques

The tall tree with glossy green leaves on the bank above the gravel path is a camphor tree (*Cinnamomum camphora*), the largest of its type ever recorded in England. It survived the winter of 2008/09 when there were prolonged temperatures of -6°C, frosts and snow which had not settled on the front lawn for over 20 years. It is native to tropical Asia, and would suffer badly if the temperature were to drop below 10°C. However, it has thrived here for more than 100 years, due to the extraordinary microclimate that also allows other tender plants to survive without winter protection.

A hidden gem

Continue along the gravel path, heading through the stone pillars at the far end. This area is known as the Secret Garden, one of many hidden corners at Overbeck's. By the end of the summer, the huge Japanese grapevine (*Vitis coignetiae*) adorning the railing has grown to make a trailing curtain. Moving past the tall date palm in the middle of the grass area, go towards the wall and look over.

Did you know?

The elegant bronze figure of a young girl was created by the Dublin-born sculptor Albert Bruce Joy (1842–1924). His other works are on display in the Houses of Parliament and Westminster Abbey.

Local legend suggests that a small bird sculpted in the girl's outstretched hand was 'shot' by US soldiers stationed at Overbeck's during the Second World War, as they used the garden for target practice. This may or may not be true, but an engraving of the statue published in the 1879 *London Art Journal* does show a small bird about to take wing from the girl's hand.

Oranges and lemons…

Below is a working greenhouse, the gardeners' bothy with a terracotta-tiled roof in the Mediterranean style, and a parterre with clipped box hedging which is cut twice a year by hand, taking a gardener two weeks to complete. This was planted in 1991 and established itself quickly. Orange and lemon trees have been planted around the outer edges and in the centre to create interest.

Retrace your steps back through the Statue Garden, but this time, as you leave, take the path that leads upwards to your left. This takes you past a rare Himalayan *Euonymus lucidus* tree on your right with leaves of red, yellow and green, and a view of the estuary framed by the branches. To the left, a vigorous Japanese wisteria (*Wisteria macrobotrys*) trained along the railings cascades dark blue flowers in the early summer.

Opposite **The Statue Garden**

Left **The Paterre**

The Upper Gardens

The Gazebo Garden

At the top of the path, there is a short flight of slate steps leading down to the Gazebo Garden. There is another sweeping view of the estuary from here, and a small sheltered seating area surrounded by two varieties of rosemary. The Riviera theme returns once more, with plantings of cistus and myrtle trees with cinnamon bark.

The Rock Dell

Going back up the steps and walking straight on takes you into the Rock Dell. The spiky plantings of phormiums, astelias, cordylines and fascicularias are softened by a profusion of luscious purple-leaved cannas, combined with the succulent purple leaves of tall aeoniums.

The jagged rock face that is exposed here is a reminder that the garden has been created on a rugged cliff. This is also one of the reasons it is possible to grow such a wide range of tender plants throughout the garden. The millions of minute rock particles from the cliff side mean that the soil is very free-draining, stopping the plants from rotting in excessively wet conditions.

Take the steps up to the picnic area, the highest point of the garden. Walk up the hill to find the most spectacular views of the coastline and estuary.

Right The Rock Dell

The Banana Garden

An oasis of calm

There is yet another small garden on the terrace below the bananas, reached via the stone steps. It is a tranquil corner, where citrus fruits are to be found in the summer, a good place to sit for a while as the scents of orange and lemon blossom drift all around.

Right Banana plant

Opposite The Banana Garden

Walk back down, through the Rock Dell, taking the steep path to your right. Rather than return to the house, follow the path right around the curve until you come to an archway. Here you suddenly find yourself in a little jungle, surrounded by high stone walls and filled with ferns and lush green foliage.

This is the most sheltered part of the garden, and is home to some of the Overbeck's most tender tropical plants. These include species fuchsias from South America, hedychiums, tree ferns (*Dicksonia antartica*) and a good number of different types of bananas. Many of these were grown from seed at Overbeck's and introduced to the Banana Garden in 2002 to extend the range of plants in the garden. These plants have been grown here since the early 1920s, and several of the stems bear fruit each year. The small green bananas are not edible, but the flowers can be eaten.

The bananas are one of the few plants that need some added protection. Each winter, the stems are wrapped in fleece to keep some warmth in, and then covered with a green mesh overcoat to keep some of the rain out.

Another significant tree nearby is the 'oven's wattle' (*Acacia pravissima*), growing against the wall by the archway, probably the largest of its kind in England, and smothered in fragrant yellow flowers each spring.

Right Ulric Hopkins in the Banana Garden, *c*.1906

The Palm Garden

Turn back and take the path out through the archway, heading down the long straight path. To your left, there is a gravelled bank filled with ornamental grasses, agaves and yuccas, as well as various restios from South Africa. The tall trees are Chusan palms (*Trachycarpus fortunei*), and are to be found throughout the garden, most dating back to the 1930s.

As you move along the path, to the right you will see that there is a series of narrow terraces, where exotic flowering shrubs are growing – banksias, proteas and pseudopanax species.

Did you know?
We now have a new weather station in action. Situated in the Orangery in the Banana Garden, it records weather data throughout the year.

Right **The Palm Garden**

Magnolias

Overbeck's has an excellent collection of *Magnolia campbellii* 'Overbeck's'. The species was first collected by Joseph Hooker in the Himalayas in 1849. There can be great variations of this magnolia, but the tree at Overbeck's has long been recognised as an extraordinary example, with its beautiful deep pink flowers in mid-February.

In late 2006, twelve new specimens were propagated, and the tree was formally renamed, so that when the original eventually dies, there will be live material to create new plants. Hopefully, smaller versions will start to appear in gardens around the world – indeed, a specimen of *Magnolia campbellii* 'Overbeck's' has already been planted in Japan.

Did you know?
The oldest living resident at Overbeck's is the famous *Magnolia campbellii* 'Overbeck's' which was planted in the garden in 1901. Although it tipped over during the winter of 1999 after heavy rain, it continues to show healthy growth.

The Woodland Garden

Further on down the path, there is a row of lantern trees (*Crinodendron hookerianum*), from Chile.

Keep going along the path until you reach the shade. Overbeck's is no more than three hectares, but it is unusual and intricate, with many different hidden aspects and surprises – it even has its own small woodland and a belvedere look-out where the trees provide framed views of both the estuary and sea. The older trees are mostly beech and evergreen oak, predating the house and garden and providing shelter from cold north winds. The grass has been left to grow longer to encourage more wildlife and to create a wildflower meadow.

As you leave up the drive, look back and you will see the large specimens of Japanese dogwood (*Cornus kousa*), poor man's umbrella (*Gunnera manicata*) and the tulip tree (*Liriodendron tulipifera*).

Our volunteer gardeners planted more than a thousand *Allium* 'Purple Sensation', *Allium multibulbosum*, *Tulipa* 'White Triumphator' and *Tulipa* 'Jan Reus' bulbs in November 2008, to create colour in the garden.

Left *Magnolia campbellii* 'Overbeck's'

Wonderful Views and Walks

The National Trust cares for thirteen miles of coastline around Salcombe and the Kingsbridge Estuary. To the east lies Prawle Point, an important landfall for migrating birds, and to the west the rugged stretch of headlands and coves extends six miles to Hope Cove. There is a network of coastal walks, and details of two suggested walks between Overbeck's and Bolt Head are given in a booklet available in the shop.

Crossing the Bar

Sunset and evening star,
And one clear call for me!
And may there be no moaning of the bar,
When I put out to sea,
But such a tide as moving seems asleep,
Too full for sound and foam,
When that which drew from out the boundless deep
Turns again home.
Twilight and evening bell,
And after that the dark!
And may there be no sadness of farewell,
When I embark;
For tho' from out our bourne of Time and Place
The flood may bear me far,
I hope to see my pilot face to face
When I have crossed the bar.

By Alfred Lord Tennyson 1889
written when staying at Salcombe